MW01178085

River and Sea Homes

Debbie Gallagher

Smart Apple Media

This edition first published in 2008 in the United States of America by Smart Apple Media.
All rights reserved. No part of this book may be reproduced in any form or by any means without written permission from the publisher.

Smart Apple Media
2140 Howard Drive West
North Mankato, Minnesota 56003

First published in 2007 by
MACMILLAN EDUCATION AUSTRALIA PTY LTD
627 Chapel Street, South Yarra, Australia 3141

Visit our Web site at www.macmillan.com.au or go directly to www.macmillanlibrary.com.au

Associated companies and representatives throughout the world.

Copyright © Debbie Gallagher 2007

Library of Congress Cataloging-in-Publication Data

Gallagher, Debbie, 1969-
    River and sea homes / by Debbie Gallagher.
    p. cm. — (Homes around the world)
    Includes index.
    ISBN 978-1-59920-152-8
    1. Dwellings—Juvenile literature. 2. Offshore structures—Juvenile literature. 3. Boat living—
Juvenile literature. 4. Houseboats—Juvenile literature. I. Title.

    TH4890.G35 2007
    728.7'9—dc22

                                                2007004644

Edited by Angelique Campbell-Muir
Text and cover design by Christine Deering
Page layout by Domenic Lauricella
Photo research by Legend Images
Illustration by Domenic Lauricella

Printed in U.S.

Acknowledgements

The author and the publisher are grateful to the following for permission to reproduce copyright material:

Cover photograph: Bajau village © Lonely Planet Images/Eric L Wheater.

© Craig Lovell/Eagle Visions Photography/Alamy, p. 13; © TNT Magazine/Alamy, p. 26; © Jürgen Freund/AUSCAPE, pp. 6 (center), 12; © Dean Conger/CORBIS/Australian Picture Library, p. 19; © Pierre Perrin/CORBIS SYGMA/Australian Picture Library, pp. 14, 15; © Breck/Dreamstime.com, p. 30 (center left); © Brownm39/Dreamstime.com, pp. 4, 30 (bottom right); © Btmo/Dreamstime.com, p. 5; © Getty Images/Image Bank/Yann Layma, pp. 6 (top), 11; © Getty Images/Photographer's Choice/Stuart Dee, p. 8; © Francoise De Mulder/Roger Viollet/Getty Images, p. 10; © Marie Mathelin/Roger Viollet/Getty Images, p. 9; © iStockphoto.com/Maria Barbulescu, p. 20; © iStockphoto.com/Eric Bechtold, p. 30 (top right); © iStockphoto.com/Jacques Croizer, p. 30 (top left); © iStockphoto.com/spencer doane, pp. 7 (bottom), 27; © iStockphoto.com/Gavin Jung, p. 22; © iStockphoto.com/Nicola Stratford, pp. 3, 25; © Lonely Planet Images/Mark Daffey, pp. 6 (bottom), 16, 18; © Lonely Planet Images/Jane Sweeney, p. 23; © Lonely Planet Images/Eric L. Wheater, pp. 1, 17; © Mark Moxon, www.moxon.net, p. 30 (bottom left); © Michael Spencer/Saudi Aramco World/PADIA, p. 30 (center right); © Photolibrary/Robert Harding Picture Library Ltd., pp. 7 (top), 21; © Photos.com, p. 24.

While every care has been taken to trace and acknowledge copyright, the publisher tenders their apologies for any accidental infringement where copyright has proved untraceable. Where the attempt has been unsuccessful, the publisher welcomes information that would redress the situation.

Contents

Glossary words
When a word is printed in **bold**, you can look up its meaning in the glossary on page 31.

Shelter

Everyone needs shelter, as well as food and water, warmth, and protection. Homes around the world provide shelter for people.

These homes are built on a lake in Asia.

People live in many different types of homes. Some people live in homes built over water. Some people live in boats.

A yacht is a type of boat that people can live in.

River and sea homes

Water homes are found on rivers, lakes, and oceans. Some are boats. Some are **stilt** houses that stand in water.

Sampans are found on rivers and harbors in Asia.

Kabang boats are made from tree trunks.

The Bajau people live in villages of homes built on stilts.

Some water homes move from place to place. Others are **stationary**. All of them must be made of materials that last a long time in water.

The Uros build reed homes that float on Lake Titicaca in South America.

People all around the world live in houseboats.

Sampan

A sampan is a wide, flat-bottomed boat with a small cabin built on top. Sampans are found in rivers, lakes, and harbors in Asia.

Some larger sampans have sails.

A sampan is made of wood. The cabin is a frame covered with overlapping woven mats. It is steered with a single oar and a **rudder**.

front of boat

cabin

cabin doorway

oar

back of boat

A sampan is steered from the back of the boat.

Inside a sampan

The family sleeps inside the sampan cabin. They spend most of the day on the back deck. This area is used for cooking and working.

cabin

doorway to front deck

storage

wooden floor

Tools and other items are stored on the walls inside the cabin.

The cabin's roof is sometimes made longer to cover the front section of the sampan. Sampans are small homes, but the families living on them use every inch of space.

Clothes are hung on poles to dry.

Kabang

In Southeast Asia, the Moken people live in boats called kabang. Kabang are found around the many small islands in the Andaman Sea.

Many Moken live their whole lives on a kabang.

A kabang is made by carving out the middle of a tree trunk. Then a floor and roof are added. The kabang is strong, so it can withstand ocean storms.

floor boards being added

hollowed tree trunk

The hollowed tree trunk will be softened with fire to make it flatter and wider.

Inside a kabang

Inside a kabang is a stove or wood fire. Beds are **hammocks** or woven mats. Fishing gear and tools are easy to reach.

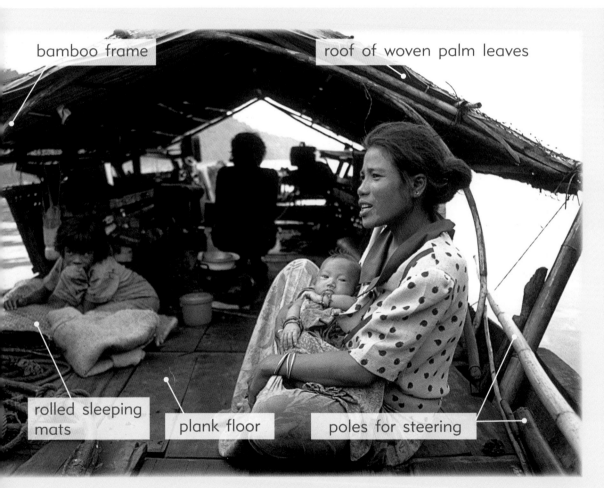

bamboo frame

roof of woven palm leaves

rolled sleeping mats

plank floor

poles for steering

An extended Moken family lives on a kabang.

The kabang is home for most of the year. Moken families travel across the sea in groups. They also travel to beaches to collect land materials.

The Moken hunt sea turtles and collect shellfish for food.

Stilt home

The Bajau people of Southeast Asia live in villages of homes built on stilts above the sea. They were once sea **nomads** who lived in boats called lepa-lepa.

Wooden paths that have been built over the sea connect the homes.

Stilt homes are made of wood, such as bamboo.
The roof is made from woven grass called thatch.

outside deck — thatch roof — window

ladder to reach boats in water — wooden stilts — fishing canoe

Bajau stilt homes are built over water so fishing is easy, even at low tide.

Inside a stilt home

Inside a stilt home there is usually one large, rectangular room. Sometimes there is also a kitchen. An outside deck adds more space.

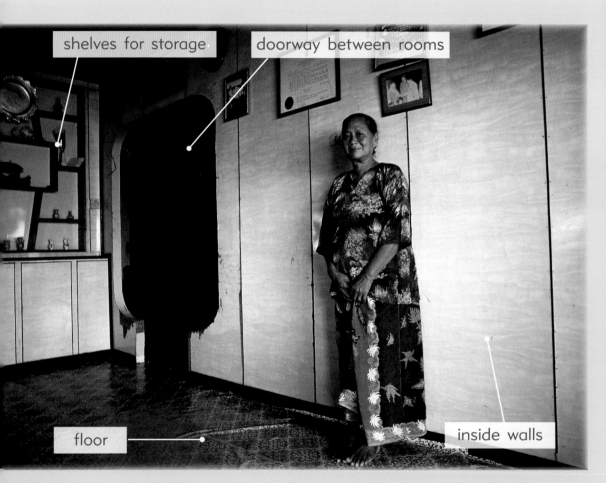

shelves for storage

doorway between rooms

inside walls

floor

This is the inside of a stilt home in Semporna, Malaysia.

Most Bajau are no longer able to live on their lepa-lepa boats. Stilt homes let the Bajau continue to live a life on the sea.

Today, lepa-lepa boats are used for fishing trips or transportation.

Floating reed home

The Uros people live in floating reed homes on Lake Titicaca in South America. The homes are made of tortora reeds that grow in the lake.

Reed homes sit on islands that the Uros made from reeds.

The Uros people use tortora reeds to make almost everything they need. Their boats, furniture, and **utensils** are made from reeds.

reed homes

tortora reeds

reed island

New reeds are added to the top of the island as the bottom rots in the water.

Inside a floating reed home

There is only one room inside a floating reed home. One corner is used as the kitchen. Door covers and bedding are made from wool.

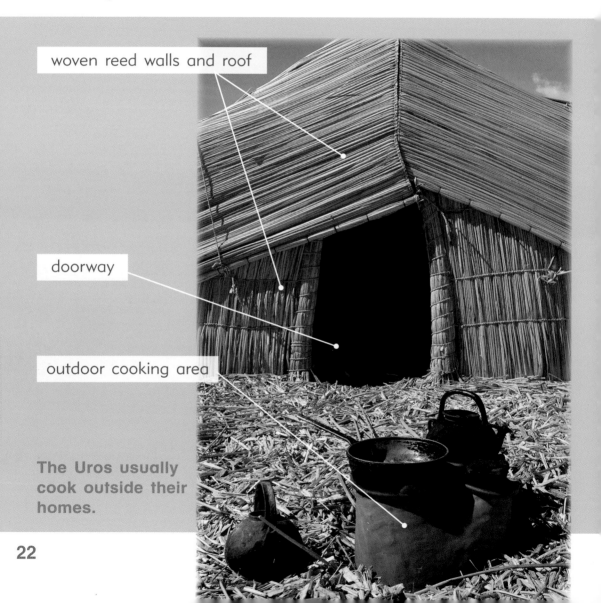

woven reed walls and roof

doorway

outdoor cooking area

The Uros usually cook outside their homes.

There are about 35 reed islands on Lake Titicaca. Most float around the lake, but some are held in one place.

Reed boats are used to travel around the lake and for fishing.

Houseboat

A houseboat is a boat that people live in. Houseboats are found in calm water such as rivers, lakes, and canals.

Families all around the world live in houseboats.

Houseboats are made from materials such as metal, wood, or **fiberglass**. The boat's shape helps it float. Ladders reach the deck on the roof of the houseboat.

upper deck

front deck

lower deck

windows

deck rails

Houseboats have engines to move them across the water.

Inside a houseboat

Inside a houseboat there is a sleeping area and a bathroom. The kitchen is called a galley. There is also a seat and a window for the driver.

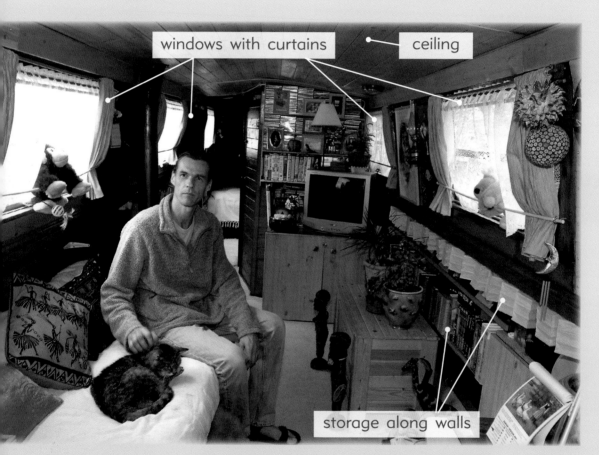

windows with curtains

ceiling

storage along walls

Batteries are used to power electrical items including televisions.

To keep a houseboat in one place, an anchor can be dropped over the side into the water. Houseboats can also be **moored** along a river or canal bank.

Some houseboats are permanently moored on city waterways.

Floor plan

This is the **floor plan** of a houseboat. It gives you a "bird's-eye view" of the rooms inside the home.

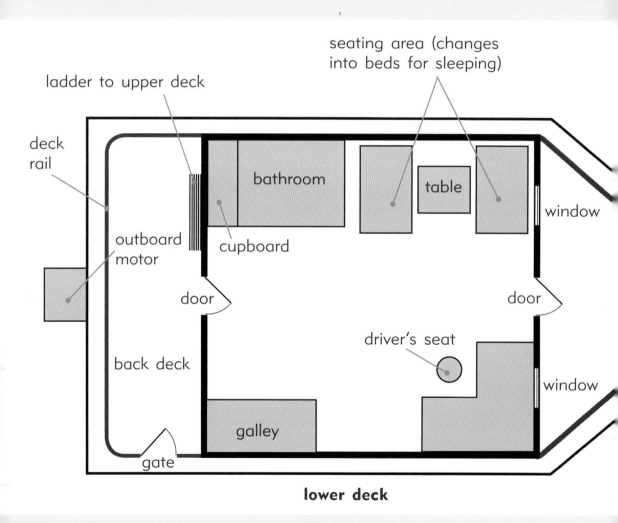

ladder to upper deck

seating area (changes into beds for sleeping)

deck rail

bathroom

table

window

outboard motor

cupboard

door

door

driver's seat

back deck

window

galley

gate

lower deck

Try this!

Draw a floor plan of your home. Label all the spaces, inside and outside, as well as features such as doors and windows.

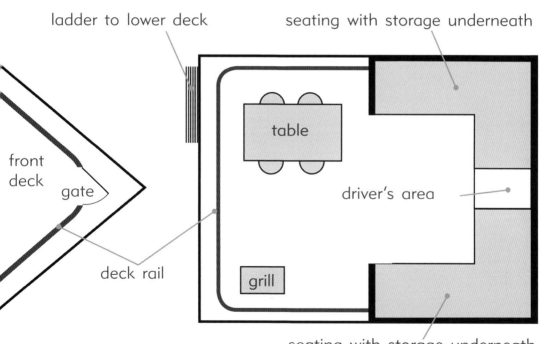

ladder to lower deck

seating with storage underneath

front deck

gate

deck rail

table

driver's area

grill

seating with storage underneath

upper deck

Homes around the world

There are many different types of homes around the world. All homes provide shelter for the people who live in them.

A pit home in Africa

New York City apartments

Windsor Castle in London

Mud and grass homes

Tuareg tent in the
Sahara Desert

Lake home in Asia

Glossary

fiberglass   material made of fine glass fibers

floor plan   a drawing that shows the layout of the areas in a home or building, as if seen from above

hammocks   hanging beds made from material

moored   held in one place by an anchor, a cable, or a secure object on land

nomads   people who move from place to place

rudder   a flat moveable object at the back of a boat, used for steering

stationary   not moving

stilt   a tall post or pole that supports a building

utensils   instruments, tools, or containers

Index